16 designs in **Luxury Cotton DK**
by Martin Storey

Classic **Art** evokes the faded elegance of an artist's studio in a London Regency Villa. As she paints she captures the beauty of her muse in oils on canvas – dreamlike days in contemplation.

The patterns in this brochure have been influenced by the Bloomsbury set and the Arts and Crafts movement. A time when women contributed to the creative arts in so many ways, breaking new ground and defying conventions.

The look is classic and serene with jumpers and cardigans teamed with timeless accessories. Garments are knitted or crocheted, cabled and striped with some tied at the waist to create an elegant line. Add a long scarf, an intriguing pendant, elegant cuffs or a witty Gingerbread cottage bag to complete the look.

Classic Art sees the launch of a new yarn for RYC, Luxury Cotton, a silky and sophisticated cotton/viscose blend. The colour palette chosen by the artist is inspired by water-colours in muted pastels and striking mid tones.

Classic Art is for the creative woman looking for understated luxury.

classicart

RYC Classic is for the woman who is looking to enhance a contemporary wardrobe with classically beautiful garments and accessories. Classic Art evokes the 1930s, the era of the creative free spirit, where new shapes and textures entered our wardrobes for the first time. Here you can relive this spirit of adventure.

The Muse who comes each morning
   In rozy gauze is clad;
Her head is crowned with flowers,
   Her eyes are clear and glad.
She is the gentle Goddess
   Who rules the dreams of youth;
Her wonderful sweet stories
   Are truer than the truth.

Muses by Victor James Daley

Georgina – an easy cable and picot lace top which wraps softly at the hip
Knitted in Luxury Cotton DK, shown here in Marble. Pattern instructions page 42

Artist Coat – different stitch textures give our three quarter length coat an unconstructed feel.
The feature belt completes the look.
Knitted in Luxury Cotton DK, shown here with Painter scarf in Tang, Damsel, Crisp & Broncho. Pattern instructions page 34

Damask – fastening at the waist, our cardigan has a garter stitch shawl collar to contrast with the cable and eyelet pattern on the body.
Knitted in Luxury Cotton DK, shown opposite in Broncho. Pattern instructions page 39

Painter scarf – an individual scarf with a chevron stripe.
Knitted in Luxury Cotton DK, shown here in Tang, Damsel, Crisp & Broncho. Pattern instructions page 56

She walks in beauty, like the night
Of cloudless climes and starry skies;
And all that's best of dark and bright
Meet in her aspect and her eyes

She Walks In Beauty by Lord George Gordon Byron

**Bohemian stripe – an easy to wear
semi fitted striped jumper**

Knitted in Luxury Cotton DK, shown here in Marble
Tang, Crisp & Broncho. Pattern instructions page 48

Vanessa – a delicate wrap effect jumper, fitted with a deep rib
Knitted in Luxury Cotton DK, shown opposite in Damsel. Pattern instructions page 46

Bloomsbury necklace and bracelet – a delicious mixture of knitted rose florets
decorated with beads
Knitted in Luxury Cotton DK, shown here in Slipper, Damsel & Broncho. Pattern instructions page 51

Landscape – our wide necked sleeveless vest is striped in delicate watercolours

Knitted in Luxury Cotton DK, shown in Marble, Damsel, Broncho & Crisp [shown here with Florence].

Pattern instructions page 44

Florence – this simple shrug has a loose rib and a flirty detail on the sleeve
Knitted in Luxury Cotton DK, shown here in Tang. Pattern instructions page 45

Cherry bright brooch – a witty crocheted cherry brooch
Knitted in Luxury Cotton DK, shown opposite in Slipper. Pattern instructions page 53

Gingerbread cottage bag – a bag full of fun decorated with roses round the door and window boxes in French knot, backstitch and lazy daisy stitch embroidery.
Knitted in Luxury Cotton DK, shown in Marble, Slipper, Damsel, Broncho, Tang, Crisp, & Char. Pattern instructions page 54

Artisan cuff – this coin cable cuff is embellished with pearl buttons.
Knitted in Luxury Cotton DK, shown in Damsel. Pattern instructions page 50

Studio pendant – a knitted spiral decorated with crystals makes a precious pendant
Knitted in Luxury Cotton DK, shown here in Crisp. Pattern instructions page 56

Love pendant – embellish this heart shaped pendant with delicate bugle beads.
Knitted in Luxury Cotton DK, shown opposite in Marble [with Studio pendant & Artisan cuff].
Pattern instructions page 52

Antique – daisy flowers
and crystals adorn this
simple striped jacket with
short sleeves.

Knitted in Luxury Cotton DK,
shown in Crisp & Pagoda.
Pattern instructions page 36

Under the arch of Life, where love and death,
Terror and mystery, guard her shrine, I saw
Beauty enthroned;

Soul's Beauty by Dante Gabriel Rossetti

Charleston – this diagonally striped scarf is fashionably long

Knitted in Luxury Cotton DK, shown in Crisp & Tang. Pattern instructions page 41

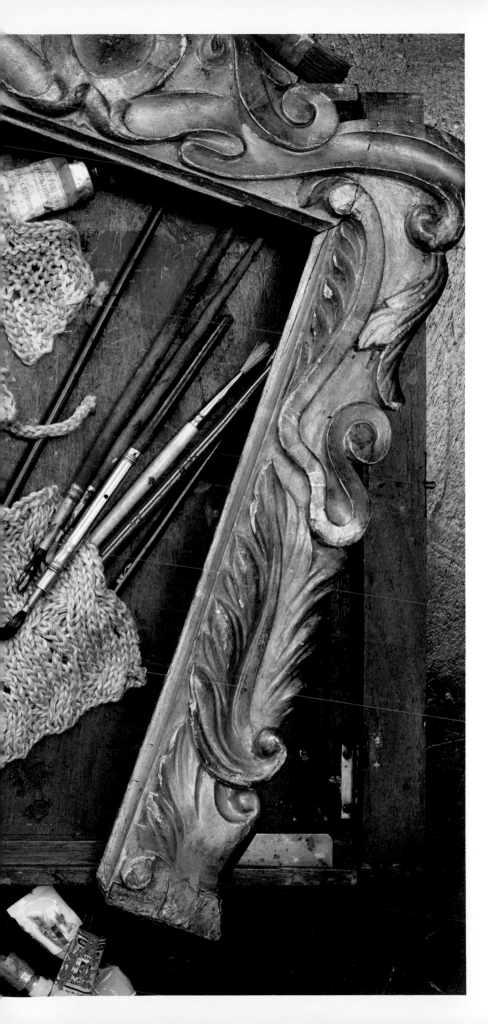

Tension

Obtaining the correct tension is perhaps the single factor which can make the difference between a successful garment and a disastrous one. It controls both the shape and size of an article, so any variation, however slight, can distort the finished garment. Different designers feature in our books and it is **their** tension, given at the **start** of each pattern, which you must match. We recommend that you knit a square in pattern and/or stocking stitch (depending on the pattern instructions) of perhaps 5 - 10 more stitches and 5 - 10 more rows than those given in the tension note. Mark out the central 10cm square with pins. If you have too many stitches to 10cm try again using thicker needles, if you have too few stitches to 10cm try again using finer needles. Once you have achieved the correct tension your garment will be knitted to the measurements indicated in the size diagram shown at the end of the pattern.

Sizing and Size Diagram Note

The instructions are given for the smallest size. Where they vary, work the figures in brackets for the larger sizes. **One set of figures refers to all sizes.** Included with most patterns in this magazine is a **'size diagram'**, or sketch of the finished garment and its dimensions. The size diagram shows the finished width of the garment at the under-arm point, and it is this measurement that the knitter should choose first; a useful tip is to measure one of your own garments which is a comfortable fit. Having chosen a size based on width, look at the corresponding length for that size; if you are not happy with the total length which we recommend, adjust your own garment before beginning your armhole shaping - any adjustment after this point will mean that your sleeve will not fit into your garment easily - don't forget to take your adjustment into account if there is any side seam shaping. Finally, look at the sleeve length; the size diagram shows the finished sleeve measurement, taking into account any top-arm insertion length. Measure your body between the centre of your neck and your wrist, this measurement should correspond to half the garment width plus the sleeve length. Again, your sleeve length may be adjusted, but remember to take into consideration your sleeve increases if you do adjust the length - you must increase more frequently than the pattern states to shorten your sleeve, less frequently to lengthen it.

Chart Note

Many of the patterns in the book are worked from charts. Each square on a chart represents a stitch and each line of squares a row of knitting. Each colour used is given a different letter and these are shown in the **materials** section, or in the **key** alongside the chart of each pattern. When working from the charts, read odd rows (K) from right to left and even rows (P) from left to right, unless otherwise stated.

Knitting with colour

There are two main methods of working colour into a knitted fabric: **Intarsia** and **Fairisle** techniques. The first method produces a single thickness of fabric and is usually used where a colour is only required in a particular area of a row and does not form a repeating pattern across the row, as in the fairisle technique.
Intarsia: The simplest way to do this is to cut short lengths of yarn for each motif or block of colour used in a row. Then joining in the various colours at the appropriate point on the row, link one colour to the next by twisting them around each other where they meet on the wrong side to avoid gaps. All ends can then either be darned along the colour join lines, as each motif is completed or then can be "knitted-in" to the fabric of the knitting as each colour is worked into the pattern. This is done in much the same way as "weaving-in" yarns when working the Fairisle technique and does save time darning-in ends. It is essential that the tension is noted for **Intarsia** as this may vary from the stocking stitch if both are used in the same pattern.
Fairisle type knitting: When two or three colours are worked repeatedly across a row, strand the yarn **not** in use loosely behind the stitches being worked. If you are working with more than two colours, treat the "floating" yarns as if they were one yarn and always spread the stitches to their correct width to keep them elastic. It is advisable not to carry the stranded or "floating" yarns over more than three stitches at a time, but to weave them under and over the colour you are working. The "floating" yarns are therefore caught at the back of the work.

Finishing Instructions

After working for hours knitting a garment, it seems a great pity that many garments are spoiled because such little care is taken in the pressing and finishing process. Follow the following tips for a truly professional-looking garment.

Pressing

Block out each piece of knitting and following the instructions on the ball band press the garment pieces, omitting the ribs. Tip: Take special care to press the edges, as this will make sewing up both easier and neater. If the ball band indicates that the fabric is not to be pressed, then covering the blocked out fabric with a damp white cotton cloth and leaving it to stand will have the desired effect. Darn in all ends neatly along the selvage edge or a colour join, as appropriate.

Stitching

When stitching the pieces together, remember to match areas of colour and texture very carefully where they meet. Use a seam stitch such as back stitch or mattress stitch for all main knitting seams and join all ribs and neckband with mattress stitch, unless otherwise stated.

Construction

Having completed the pattern instructions, join left shoulder and neckband seams as detailed above. Sew the top of the sleeve to the body of the garment using the method detailed in the pattern, referring to the appropriate guide:

Set-in sleeves: Place centre of cast-off edge of sleeve to shoulder seam. Set in sleeve, easing sleeve head into armhole.

Straight cast-off sleeves: Place centre of cast-off edge of sleeve to shoulder seam. Sew top of sleeve to body.

Join side and sleeve seams.
Slip stitch pocket edgings and linings into place.
Sew on buttons to correspond with buttonholes.
Ribbed welts and neckbands and any area of garter stitch should not be pressed.

Abbreviations

K	knit	sl 2	slip two stitches
P	purl	psso	pass slipped
st(s)	stitch(es)		stitch over
inc	increase(e)(ing)	tbl	through back
dec	decrease(e)(ing)		of loop
st st	stocking stitch	M1	make one stitch
	(1 row K, 1 row P)		by picking up
g st	garter stitch		horizontal loop
	(K every row)		before next stitch
beg	begin(ning)		and working into
foll	following		back of it
rem	remain(ing)	yrn	yarn round needle
rep	repeat	yfwd	yarn forward
alt	alternate	yon	yarn over needle
cont	continue	yfrn	yarn forward and
patt	pattern		round needle
tog	together	meas	measures
mm	millimetres	o	no stitches,
cm	centimetres		times, or rows
in(s)	inch(es)	-	no stitches, times
RS	right side		or rows for that
WS	wrong side		size
sl 1	slip one stitch	approx	approximately

Crochet terms

UK crochet terms and abbreviation have been used throughout. The list below gives the US equivalent where they vary.

Abbrev.	UK	US
dc	double crochet	single crochet
htr	half treble	half double crochet
tr	treble	double crochet
dtr	double treble	treble crochet

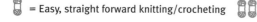 = Easy, straight forward knitting/crocheting   = Suitable for the average knitter   = For the more experienced knitter

YARN

	XS	S	M	L	XL	
To fit bust	81	86	91	97	102	cm
	32	34	36	38	40	in

RYC Luxury Cotton DK

A Broncho	256	9	10	10	11	11	x 50gm
B Crisp	253	3	3	3	3	3	x 50gm
C Tang	252	3	3	3	3	4	x 50gm
D Damsel	251	5	6	6	6	6	x 50gm

NEEDLES

1 pair 3¼mm (no 10) (US 3) needles
1 pair 4mm (no 8) (US 6) needles
3¼mm (no 10) (US 3) circular needle

TENSION

22 sts and 30 rows to 10 cm measured over stocking stitch using 4mm (US 6) needles.

SPECIAL ABBREVIATIONS

cluster 3 = K3, lift first of these 3 sts over 2nd and 3rd sts and off right needle; **net 3** = sl 2 as though to K2tog, lift first of these 2 sts over 2nd st and off right needle, sl 1, now lift previous st on right needle over this st and off right needle, slip same st back onto left needle, (yfwd) twice – to make 2 sts, K1.

BACK

Using 3¼mm (US 3) needles and yarn A cast on 108 [114: 120: 126: 132] sts.
**Work in g st for 2 rows.
Join in yarn B.
Using yarn B, work in g st for 2 rows.
Join in yarn C.
Using yarn C, work in g st for 2 rows.
Join in yarn D.
Using yarn D, work in g st for 2 rows, ending with RS facing for next row.
Change to 4mm (US 6) needles.**
Row 1 (RS): Using yarn B, knit.
Row 2: Using yarn B, P1, *K2tog, rep from * to last st, P1.
Row 3: Using yarn B, K1, inc once in each st to last st, K1.
Row 4: Using yarn B, purl.
Rows 5 to 8: As rows 1 to 4 **but using yarn A**.
Rows 9 to 12: As rows 1 to 4 **but using yarn C**.

Rows 13 to 16: As rows 1 to 4 **but using yarn D**.
Row 17: Using yarn D, K2, *yfwd, cluster 3, rep from * to last st, K1.
Row 18: Using yarn A, purl.
Row 19: Using yarn A, K1, *cluster 3, yfwd, rep from * to last 2 sts, K2.
Row 20: Using yarn D, purl.
Rows 21 to 24: As rows 17 to 20.
Rows 25 and 26: As rows 17 and 18.
Row 27: Using yarn A, K2, *net 3, rep from * to last st, K1.
Row 28: Using yarn A, K3, *P1, K2, rep from * to end.
Rows 29 to 34: As rows 27 and 28, 3 times.
These 34 rows form patt.
Cont in patt until back meas 75 [76: 77: 78: 79] cm, ending with RS facing for next row.
Shape shoulders and back neck
Cast off 11 [12: 13: 14: 15] sts at beg of next 2 rows. 86 [90: 94: 98: 102] sts.
Next row (RS): Cast off 11 [12: 13: 14: 15] sts, patt until there are 16 [16: 17: 17: 18] sts on right needle and turn, leaving rem sts on a holder.
Work each side of neck separately.
Cast off 4 sts at beg of next row.
Cast off rem 12 [12: 13: 13: 14] sts.
With RS facing, rejoin appropriate yarn to rem sts, cast off centre 32 [34: 34: 36: 36] sts, patt to end.
Complete to match first side, reversing shapings.

LEFT FRONT

Using 3¼mm (US 3) needles and yarn A cast on 57 [60: 63: 66: 69] sts.
Work as given for back from ** to **.
Row 1 (RS): Using yarn B, knit.
Row 2: Using yarn B, P2 [1: 2: 1: 2], *K2tog, rep from * to last st, P1.
Row 3: Using yarn B, K1, inc once in each st to last 2 [1: 2: 1: 2] sts, K2 [1: 2: 1: 2].
Row 4: Using yarn B, purl.
Rows 5 to 8: As rows 1 to 4 **but using yarn A**.
Rows 9 to 12: As rows 1 to 4 **but using yarn C**.
Rows 13 to 16: As rows 1 to 4 **but using yarn D**.
Row 17: Using yarn D, K2, *yfwd, cluster 3, rep from * to last st, K1.
Row 18: Using yarn A, purl.
Row 19: Using yarn A, K1, *cluster 3, yfwd, rep from * to last 2 sts, K2.

Row 20: Using yarn D, purl.
Rows 21 to 24: As rows 17 to 20.
Rows 25 and 26: As rows 17 and 18.
Row 27: Using yarn A, K2, *net 3, rep from * to last st, K1.
Row 28: Using yarn A, K3, *P1, K2, rep from * to end.
Rows 29 to 34: As rows 27 and 28, 3 times.
These 34 rows form patt.
Cont in patt until 37 [37: 37: 39: 39] rows less have been worked than on back to beg of shoulder shaping, ending with **WS** facing for next row.
Shape neck
Keeping patt correct, cast off 9 [10: 10: 10: 10] sts at beg of next row. 48 [50: 53: 56: 59] sts.
Dec 1 st at neck edge of next 7 rows, then on foll 1 [1: 1: 2: 2] alt rows, then on every foll 4th row until 34 [36: 39: 41: 44] sts rem.
Work 3 rows, ending with RS facing for next row.
Shape shoulder
Cast off 11 [12: 13: 14: 15] sts at beg of next and foll alt row.
Work 1 row.
Cast off rem 12 [12: 13: 13: 14] sts.

RIGHT FRONT

Work to match left front, reversing shapings.

SLEEVES

Using 3¼mm (US 3) needles and yarn A cast on 96 [96: 102: 102: 108] sts.
Work as given for back from ** to **.
Beg with row 1, cont in patt as given for back until sleeve meas 41 [41: 42: 42: 42] cm, ending with RS facing for next row.
Cast off.

MAKING UP

Press as described on the information page.
Join both shoulder seams using back stitch, or mattress stitch if preferred.
Front bands (both alike)
With RS facing, using 3¼mm (US 3) needles and yarn A, pick up and knit 138 [140: 142: 144: 146] sts evenly along front opening edge, between cast-on edge and neck shaping.
Row 1 (WS): Using yarn A, knit.
Rows 2 and 3: Using yarn B, knit.

Rows 4 and 5: Using yarn C, knit.
Rows 6 and 7: Using yarn D, knit.
Row 8 (RS): Using yarn A, knit.
Using yarn A, cast off knitwise (on **WS**).
Neckband
With RS facing, using 3¼mm (US 3) needles and yarn A, beg and ending at cast-off edges of bands, pick up and knit 49 [50: 50: 52: 52] sts up right side of neck, 40 [42: 42: 44: 44] sts from back, then 49 [50: 50: 52: 52] sts down left side of neck. 138 [142: 142: 148: 148] sts.
Row 1 (WS): Using yarn A, knit.
Rows 2 and 3: Using yarn B, knit.
Rows 4 and 5: Using yarn C, knit.
Rows 6 and 7: Using yarn D, knit.
Rows 8 and 9: Using yarn A, knit.
Rows 10 to 15: As rows 2 to 7.
Row 16 (RS): Using yarn A, knit.
Using yarn A, cast off knitwise (on **WS**).
Belt
Using 3¼mm (US 3) circular needle and yarn A cast on 380 sts.
Rows 1 and 2: Using yarn A, knit.
Rows 3 and 4: Using yarn B, knit.

Rows 5 and 6: Using yarn C, knit.
Rows 7 and 8: Using yarn D, knit.
Rows 9 to 16: As rows 1 to 8.
Row 17 (RS): Using yarn A, knit.

Using yarn A, cast off knitwise (on **WS**).
See information page for finishing instructions, setting in sleeves using the straight cast-off method.

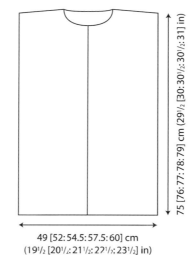

75 [76: 77: 78: 79] cm (29½ [30: 30½: 30½: 31] in)

49 [52: 54.5: 57.5: 60] cm
(19½ [20½: 21½: 22½: 23½] in)

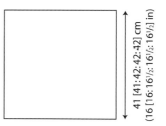

41 [41: 42: 42: 42] cm
(16 [16: 16½: 16½: 16½] in)

YARN

	XS	S	M	L	XL	
To fit bust	81	86	91	97	102	cm
	32	34	36	38	40	in

RYC Luxury Cotton DK

A Crisp	253	5	5	6	6	6	x 50gm
B Pagoda	255	4	4	4	5	5	x 50gm

NEEDLES

1 pair 3¼mm (no 10) (US 3) needles
1 pair 4mm (no 8) (US 6) needles

BUTTONS – 6 x 00322

BEADS – approx 190 [190: 230: 230: 240] clear round – ref 01008, available from Rowan Yarns and 950 [950: 1,150: 1,150: 1,200] large bugle beads – ref GB11 colour 1F. Crystal, available from Creative Beadcraft Ltd.

TENSION

22 sts and 30 rows to 10 cm measured over stocking stitch using 4mm (US 6) needles.

SPECIAL ABBREVIATION

Bead 1 = place a bead by bringing yarn to RS of work and slipping bead up next to st just worked, slip next st purlwise from left needle to right needle and take yarn to appropriate side of work for next st, leaving bead sitting on RS of work in front of slipped st. Do not place beads on edge stitches of work as this will interfere with seaming.

Pattern note: Before starting to knit, thread clear round beads onto yarn. To do this, thread a fine sewing needle (one that will easily pass through the beads) with sewing thread. Knot ends of thread and then pass end of yarn through this loop. Thread a bead onto sewing thread and then gently slide it along and onto knitting yarn. Continue in this way until required number of beads are on yarn.

BACK

Using 3¼mm (US 3) needles and yarn A cast on 95 [101: 107: 113: 119] sts.

Work in g st for 2 rows, ending with RS facing for next row.

Change to 4mm (US 6) needles.

Row 1 (RS): Using yarn A, knit.

Row 2: Using yarn A, purl.

Rows 3 and 4: As rows 1 and 2.

Row 5: As row 1.

Row 6: Using yarn A, P15 [18: 5: 8: 11], *bead 1, P15, rep from * to last 16 [19: 6: 9: 12] sts, bead 1, P to end.

Rows 7 to 10: As rows 1 and 2, twice.

Join in yarn B.

Row 11: Using yarn B, K2tog, K to last 2 sts, K2tog. 93 [99: 105: 111: 117] sts.

Row 12: Using yarn B, purl.

Row 13: Using yarn B, knit.

Rows 14 and 15: As rows 12 and 13.

Row 16: Using yarn B, P6 [9: 12: 15: 18], *bead 1, P15, rep from * to last 7 [10: 13: 16: 19] sts, bead 1, P to end.

Row 17: As row 13.

Row 18: As row 12.

Row 19: As row 11. 91 [97: 103: 109: 115] sts.

Row 20: As row 12.

These 20 rows form patt and beg side seam shaping.

Cont in patt, shaping side seams by dec 1 st at each end of 7th and every foll 6th row until 85 [91: 97: 103: 109] sts rem.

Work 9 rows, ending with RS facing for next row.

Inc 1 st at each end of next and every foll 10th row until there are 95 [101: 107: 113: 119] sts, taking inc sts into patt.

Work 5 [9: 9: 11: 11] rows, ending after patt row 14 [18: 18: 20: 20] and with RS facing for next row. (Back should meas 32 [33: 33: 34: 34] cm.)

Shape armholes

Keeping patt correct, cast off 5 [6: 6: 7: 7] sts at beg of next 2 rows. 85 [89: 95: 99: 105] sts.

Dec 1 st at each end of next 5 [5: 7: 7: 9] rows, then on foll 1 [2: 2: 3: 3] alt rows, then on foll 4th row. 71 [73: 75: 77: 79] sts.

Cont straight until armhole meas 20 [20: 21: 21: 22] cm, ending with RS facing for next row.

Shape shoulders and back neck

Cast off 7 sts at beg of next 2 rows.

57 [59: 61: 63: 65] sts.

Next row (RS): Cast off 7 sts, patt until there are 10 [10: 11: 11: 12] sts on right needle and turn, leaving rem sts on a holder.

Work each side of neck separately.

Cast off 4 sts at beg of next row.

Cast off rem 6 [6: 7: 7: 8] sts.

With RS facing, rejoin appropriate yarn to rem sts, cast off centre 23 [25: 25: 27: 27] sts, patt to end.

Complete to match first side, reversing shapings.

LEFT FRONT

Using 3¼mm (US 3) needles and yarn A cast on 48 [51: 54: 57: 60] sts.

Work in g st for 2 rows, ending with RS facing for next row.

Change to 4mm (US 6) needles.

Row 1 (RS): Using yarn A, knit.

Row 2: Using yarn A, purl.

Rows 3 and 4: As rows 1 and 2.

Row 5: As row 1.

Row 6: Using yarn A, P16, *bead 1, P15, rep from * to last 16 [19: 6: 9: 12] sts, bead 1, P to end.

Rows 7 to 10: As rows 1 and 2, twice.

Join in yarn B.

Row 11: Using yarn B, K2tog, K to end. 47 [50: 53: 56: 59] sts.

Row 12: Using yarn B, purl.

Row 13: Using yarn B, knit.

Rows 14 and 15: As rows 12 and 13.

Row 16: Using yarn B, P8, *bead 1, P15, rep from * to last 7 [10: 13: 16: 19] sts, bead 1, P to end.

Row 17: As row 13.

Row 18: As row 12.

Row 19: As row 11. 46 [49: 52: 55: 58] sts.

Row 20: As row 12.

These 20 rows form patt and beg side seam shaping.

Cont in patt, shaping side seams by dec 1 st at beg of 7th and every foll 6th row until 43 [46: 49: 52: 55] sts rem.

Work 9 rows, ending with RS facing for next row.

Inc 1 st at beg of next and every foll 10th row until there are 48 [51: 54: 57: 60] sts, taking inc sts into patt.

Cont straight until left front matches back to beg

of armhole shaping, ending with RS facing for next row.

Shape armhole
Keeping patt correct, cast off 5 [6: 6: 7: 7] sts at beg of next row. 43 [45: 48: 50: 53] sts.
Work 1 row.
Dec 1 st at armhole edge of next 5 [5: 7: 7: 9] rows, then on foll 1 [2: 2: 3: 3] alt rows, then on foll 4th row. 36 [37: 38: 39: 40] sts.
Cont straight until 17 [17: 17: 19: 19] rows less have been worked than on back to beg of shoulder shaping, ending with **WS** facing for next row.

Shape neck
Keeping patt correct, cast off 9 [10: 10: 10: 10] sts at beg of next row. 27 [27: 28: 29: 30] sts.
Dec 1 st at neck edge of next 3 rows, then on foll 2 [2: 2: 3: 3] alt rows, then on every foll 4th row until 20 [20: 21: 21: 22] sts rem.
Work 1 row, ending with RS facing for next row.

Shape shoulder
Cast off 7 sts at beg of next and foll alt row.
Work 1 row.
Cast off rem 6 [6: 7: 7: 8] sts.

RIGHT FRONT
Using 3¼mm (US 3) needles and yarn A cast on 48 [51: 54: 57: 60] sts.
Work in g st for 2 rows, ending with RS facing for next row.
Change to 4mm (US 6) needles.
Row 1 (RS): Using yarn A, knit.
Row 2: Using yarn A, purl.
Rows 3 and 4: As rows 1 and 2.
Row 5: As row 1.
Row 6: Using yarn A, P15 [18: 5: 8: 11], *bead 1, P15, rep from * to last 17 sts, bead 1, P16.
Rows 7 to 10: As rows 1 and 2, twice.
Join in yarn B.
Row 11: Using yarn B, K to last 2 sts, K2tog. 47 [50: 53: 56: 59] sts.
Row 12: Using yarn B, purl.
Row 13: Using yarn B, knit.
Rows 14 and 15: As rows 12 and 13.
Row 16: Using yarn B, P6 [9: 12: 15: 18], *bead 1, P15, rep from * to last 9 sts, bead 1, P8.
Row 17: As row 13.

Row 18: As row 12.
Row 19: As row 11. 46 [49: 52: 55: 58] sts.
Row 20: As row 12.
These 20 rows form patt and beg side seam shaping.
Complete to match left front, reversing shapings.

SLEEVES
Using 3¼mm (US 3) needles and yarn A cast on 61 [61: 63: 65: 67] sts.
Work in g st for 4 rows, ending with RS facing for next row.
Change to 4mm (US 6) needles.
Join in yarn B.
Row 1 (RS): Using yarn B, knit.
Row 2: Using yarn B, purl.
Rows 3 and 4: As rows 1 and 2.
Row 5: Using yarn B, inc in first st, K to last st, inc in last st.
63 [63: 65: 67: 69] sts.
Row 6: Using yarn B, P7 [7: 8: 9: 10], (bead 1, P15) 3 times, bead 1, P to end.
Rows 7 and 8: As rows 1 and 2.
Row 9: As row 5. 65 [65: 67: 69: 71] sts.
Row 10: As row 2.
Row 11: Using yarn A, Knit.
Row 12: Using yarn A, purl.
Row 13: Using yarn A, inc in first st, K to last st, inc in last st. 67 [67: 69: 71: 73] sts.
Row 14: As row 12.
Row 15: As row 11.
Row 16: Using yarn A, P17 [17: 18: 19: 20], (bead 1, P15) twice, bead 1, P to end.
Row 17: As row 13. 69 [69: 71: 73: 75] sts.
Row 18: As row 12.
Rows 19 and 20: As rows 11 and 12.
These 20 rows form patt and beg sleeve shaping.
Cont in patt, shaping sides by inc 1 st at each end of next and foll 0 [4th: 4th: 4th: 4th] row.
71 [73: 75: 77: 79] sts.
Work 3 [3: 3: 5: 5] rows, ending after patt row 4 [8: 8: 10: 10] and with RS facing for next row.
(Sleeve should meas 9 [10: 10: 11: 11] cm.)

Shape top
Keeping patt correct, cast off 5 [6: 6: 7: 7] sts at beg of next 2 rows. 61 [61: 63: 63: 65] sts.

Dec 1 st at each end of next 3 rows, then on foll 4 alt rows, then on every foll 4th row until 35 [35: 37: 37: 39] sts rem.
Work 1 row, ending with RS facing for next row.
Dec 1 st at each end of next and every foll alt row to 29 sts, then on foll 3 rows, ending with RS facing for next row.
Cast off rem 23 sts.

MAKING UP
Press as described on the information page.
Join both shoulder seams using back stitch, or mattress stitch if preferred.

Button band
Using 3¼mm (US 3) needles and yarn A cast on 7 sts.
Row 1 (RS): K2, P1, K1, P1, K2.
Row 2: K1, (P1, K1) 3 times.
These 2 rows form rib.
Cont in rib until button band, when slightly stretched, fits up left front opening edge to neck shaping, ending with RS facing for next row.
Cast off.
Slip stitch band in place.
Mark positions for 6 buttons on this band – first to come 2 cm up from cast-on edge, last to come just below neck shaping, and rem 4 buttons evenly spaced between.

Buttonhole band
Using 3¼mm (US 3) needles and yarn A cast on 7 sts.
Cont in rib as given for button band until buttonhole band, when slightly stretched, fits up right front opening edge to neck shaping, ending with RS facing for next row and with the addition of 6 buttonholes worked to correspond with positions marked for buttons as folls:
Buttonhole row (RS): Rib 3, yrn (to make a buttonhole), work 2 tog, rib 2.
When band is complete, cast off.
Slip stitch band in place.

Collar
With RS facing, using 3¼mm (US 3) needles and yarn A, beg and ending halfway across top of bands, pick up and knit 35 [36: 36: 38: 38] sts up right side of neck, 33 [35: 35: 37: 37] sts from

back, then 35 [36: 36: 38: 38] sts down left side of neck. 103 [107: 107: 113: 113] sts.

Row 1 (WS of body, RS of collar): K2, *P1, K1, rep from * to last st, K1.

Row 2: K1, *P1, K1, rep from * to end.

These 2 rows form rib.

Cont in rib until collar meas 5 cm, ending after row 2.

Next row (RS of collar): Rib 18 [18: 18: 19: 19], *inc in next st, rib 1, rep from * to last 17 [17: 17: 18: 18] sts, rib to end. 137 [143: 143: 151: 151] sts.

Beg with row 2, cont in rib until collar meas 11 cm from pick-up row.

Cast off in rib.

See information page for finishing instructions, setting in sleeves using the set-in method.

Using photograph as a guide, attach 5 bugle beads around each clear round bead to form flower shape.

52 [53: 54: 55: 56] cm
(20½ [21: 21½: 21½: 22] in)

43 [46: 48.5: 51.5: 54] cm
(17 [18: 19: 20½: 21½] in)

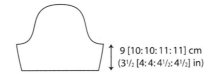

9 [10: 10: 11: 11] cm
(3½ [4: 4: 4½: 4½] in)

YARN

	XS	S	M	L	XL
To fit bust	81	86	91	97	102 cm
	32	34	36	38	40 in

RYC Luxury Cotton DK

	18	19	20	21	22 x 50gm

(photographed in Broncho 256)

NEEDLES

1 pair 3¼mm (no 10) (US 3) needles
1 pair 4mm (no 8) (US 6) needles
Cable needle

TENSION

30 sts and 30 rows to 10 cm measured over pattern using 4mm (US 6) needles.

SPECIAL ABBREVIATIONS

C6B = slip next 3 sts onto cable needle and leave at back of work, K3, then K3 from cable needle.

LEFT FRONT

Using 3¼mm (US 3) needles cast on 83 [86: 89: 92: 95] sts.
Work in g st for 5 rows, ending with **WS** facing for next row.
Row 6 (WS): K1, *(K2, M1) twice, K2, rep from * to last 4 [1: 4: 1: 4] sts, (K2, M1) 1 [0: 1: 0: 1] times, K2 [1: 2: 1: 2]. 110 [114: 118: 122: 126] sts.
Change to 4mm (US 6) needles.
Row 1 (RS): P6 [2: 6: 2: 6], *K6, P2, rep from * to end.
Row 2 and every foll alt row: K2, *P6, K2, rep from * to last 4 [0: 4: 0: 4] sts, K4 [0: 4: 0: 4].
Row 3: P6 [2: 6: 2: 6], *C6B, P2, rep from * to end.
Row 5: As row 1.
Row 7: P6 [2: 6: 2: 6], *K1, yfwd, K2tog, K3, P2, rep from * to end.
Row 9: P6 [2: 6: 2: 6], *sl 1, K1, psso, yfwd, K4, P2, rep from * to end.
Row 11: As row 7.
Row 13: As row 1.
Row 15: As row 3.
Row 17: As row 1.

Row 19: P6 [2: 6: 2: 6], *K3, sl 1, K1, psso, yfwd, K1, P2, rep from * to end.
Row 21: P6 [2: 6: 2: 6], *K4, yfwd, K2tog, P2, rep from * to end.
Row 23: As row 19.
Row 24: As row 2.
These 24 rows form patt.
Cont in patt for a further 44 rows, ending with RS facing for next row.
Shape front slope
Keeping patt correct, dec 1 st at end of next row and at same edge on foll 22 [22: 20: 18: 14] rows, then on foll 14 [15: 16: 19: 21] alt rows.
73 [76: 81: 84: 90] sts.
Work 1 row, ending with RS facing for next row.
(Left front should meas 41 [42: 42: 43: 43] cm.)
Shape armhole
Keeping patt correct, cast off 7 [8: 8: 9: 9] sts at beg and dec 1 st at end of next row.
65 [67: 72: 74: 80] sts.
Work 1 row.
Dec 1 st at armhole edge of next 7 [7: 9: 9: 11] rows, then on foll 3 [4: 4: 5: 5] alt rows, then on 2 foll 4th rows **and at same time** dec 1 st at front slope edge on next and every foll alt row.
42 [42: 44: 44: 47] sts.
Dec 1 st at front slope edge **only** on 2nd and every foll alt row until 26 [27: 29: 30: 32] sts rem.
Cont straight until armhole meas 21 [21: 22: 22: 23] cm, ending with RS facing for next row.
Shape shoulder
Cast off 9 [9: 10: 10: 11] sts at beg of next and foll alt row.
Work 1 row.
Cast off rem 8 [9: 9: 10: 10] sts.

RIGHT FRONT

Using 3¼mm (US 3) needles cast on 83 [86: 89: 92: 95] sts.
Work in g st for 5 rows, ending with **WS** facing for next row.
Row 6 (WS): K2 [1: 2: 1: 2], (M1, K2) 1 [0: 1: 0: 1] times, *(K2, M1) twice, K2, rep from * to last st, K1. 110 [114: 118: 122: 126] sts.

Change to 4mm (US 6) needles.
Row 1 (RS): P2, *K6, P2, rep from * to last 4 [0: 4: 0: 4] sts, P4 [0: 4: 0: 4].
Row 2 and every foll alt row: K6 [2: 6: 2: 6], *P6, K2, rep from * to end.
Row 3: P2, *C6B, P2, rep from * to last 4 [0: 4: 0: 4] sts, P4 [0: 4: 0: 4].
Row 5: As row 1.
Row 7: P2, *K1, yfwd, K2tog, K3, P2, rep from * to last 4 [0: 4: 0: 4] sts, P4 [0: 4: 0: 4].
Row 9: P2, *sl 1, K1, psso, yfwd, K4, P2, rep from * to last 4 [0: 4: 0: 4] sts, P4 [0: 4: 0: 4].
Row 11: As row 7.
Row 13: As row 1.
Row 15: As row 3.
Row 17: As row 1.
Row 19: P2, *K3, sl 1, K1, psso, yfwd, K1, P2, rep from * to last 4 [0: 4: 0: 4] sts, P4 [0: 4: 0: 4].
Row 21: P2, *K4, yfwd, K2tog, P2, rep from * to last 4 [0: 4: 0: 4] sts, P4 [0: 4: 0: 4].
Row 23: As row 19.
Row 24: As row 2.
These 24 rows form patt.
Cont in patt for a further 44 rows, ending with RS facing for next row.
Shape front slope
Keeping patt correct, dec 1 st at beg of next row and at same edge on foll 22 [22: 20: 18: 14] rows, then on foll 14 [15: 16: 19: 21] alt rows.
73 [76: 81: 84: 90] sts.
Complete to match left front, reversing shapings.

BACK

Using 3¼mm (US 3) needles cast on 98 [104: 110: 116: 122] sts.
Work in g st for 5 rows, ending with **WS** facing for next row.
Row 6 (WS): K2 [1: 2: 1: 2], (M1, K2) 1 [0: 1: 0: 1] times, *(K2, M1) twice, K2, rep from * to last 4 [1: 4: 1: 4] sts, (K2, M1) 1 [0: 1: 0: 1] times, K2 [1: 2: 1: 2]. 130 [138: 146: 154: 162] sts.
Change to 4mm (US 6) needles.
Row 1 (RS): P6 [2: 6: 2: 6], *K6, P2, rep from * to last 4 [0: 4: 0: 4] sts, P4 [0: 4: 0: 4].

Row 2 and every foll alt row: K6 [2: 6: 2: 6], *P6, K2, rep from * to last 4 [0: 4: 0: 4] sts, K4 [0: 4: 0: 4].

Row 3: P6 [2: 6: 2: 6], *C6B, P2, rep from * to last 4 [0: 4: 0: 4] sts, P4 [0: 4: 0: 4].

Row 5: As row 1.

Row 7: P6 [2: 6: 2: 6], *K1, yfwd, K2tog, K3, P2, rep from * to last 4 [0: 4: 0: 4] sts, P4 [0: 4: 0: 4].

Row 9: P6 [2: 6: 2: 6], *sl 1, K1, psso, yfwd, K4, P2, rep from * to last 4 [0: 4: 0: 4] sts, P4 [0: 4: 0: 4].

Row 11: As row 7.

Row 13: As row 1.

Row 15: As row 3.

Row 17: As row 1.

Row 19: P6 [2: 6: 2: 6], *K3, sl 1, K1, psso, yfwd, K1, P2, rep from * to last 4 [0: 4: 0: 4] sts, P4 [0: 4: 0: 4].

Row 21: P6 [2: 6: 2: 6], *K4, yfwd, K2tog, P2, rep from * to last 4 [0: 4: 0: 4] sts, P4 [0: 4: 0: 4].

Row 23: As row 19.

Row 24: As row 2.

These 24 rows form patt.

Cont in patt until back matches fronts to beg of armhole shaping, ending with RS facing for next row.

Shape armholes

Keeping patt correct, cast off 7 [8: 8: 9: 9] sts at beg of next 2 rows. 116 [122: 130: 136: 144] sts.

Dec 1 st at each end of next 7 [7: 9: 9: 11] rows, then on foll 3 [4: 4: 5: 5] alt rows, then on every foll 4th row until 92 [96: 100: 104: 108] sts rem.

Cont straight until back matches fronts to beg of shoulder shaping, ending with RS facing for next row.

Shape shoulders and back neck

Cast off 9 [9: 10: 10: 11] sts at beg of next 2 rows. 74 [78: 80: 84: 86] sts.

Next row (RS): Cast off 9 [9: 10: 10: 11] sts, patt until there are 12 [13: 13: 14: 14] sts on right needle and turn, leaving rem sts on a holder.

Work each side of neck separately.

Cast off 4 sts at beg of next row.

Cast off rem 8 [9: 9: 10: 10] sts.

With RS facing, rejoin yarn to rem sts, cast off centre 32 [34: 34: 36: 36] sts dec 8 sts evenly, patt to end.

Complete to match first side, reversing shapings.

SLEEVES

Using 3¼mm (US 3) needles cast on 64 [64: 66: 68: 68] sts.

Work in g st for 5 rows, ending with **WS** facing for next row.

Row 6 (WS): K1 [1: 2: 3: 3], (M1, K2) twice, *(K2, M1) twice, K2, rep from * to last 5 [5: 6: 7: 7] sts, (K2, M1) twice, K1 [1: 2: 3: 3]. 86 [86: 88: 90: 90] sts.

Change to 4mm (US 6) needles.

Row 1 (RS): Po [0: 1: 2: 2], *K6, P2, rep from * to last 6 [6: 7: 8: 8] sts, K6, Po [0: 1: 2: 2].

Row 2 and every foll alt row: Ko [0: 1: 2: 2], *P6, K2, rep from * to last 6 [6: 7: 8: 8] sts, P6, Ko [0: 1: 2: 2].

Row 3: Po [0: 1: 2: 2], *C6B, P2, rep from * to last 6 [6: 7: 8: 8] sts, C6B, Po [0: 1: 2: 2].

Row 5: As row 1.

Row 7: Po [0: 1: 2: 2], *K1, yfwd, K2tog, K3, P2, rep from * to last 6 [6: 7: 8: 8] sts, K1, yfwd, K2tog, K3, Po [0: 1: 2: 2].

Row 9: Po [0: 1: 2: 2], *sl 1, K1, psso, yfwd, K4, P2, rep from * to last 6 [6: 7: 8: 8] sts, sl 1, K1, psso, yfwd, K4, Po [0: 1: 2: 2].

Row 11: As row 7.

Row 13: As row 1.

Row 15: As row 3.

Row 17: As row 1.

Row 19: Po [0: 1: 2: 2], *K3, sl 1, K1, psso, yfwd, K1, P2, rep from * to last 6 [6: 7: 8: 8] sts, K3, sl 1, K1, psso, yfwd, K1, Po [0: 1: 2: 2].

Row 20: As row 2.

These 20 rows **set position** of patt as given for back and fronts.

Cont in patt as now set, shaping sides by inc 1 st at each end of 11th [5th: 5th: 5th: next] and every foll 30th [24th: 24th: 24th: 20th] row to 94 [96: 94: 96: 98] sts, then on every foll - [-: 26th: 26th: 22nd]

row until there are - [-: 98: 100: 102] sts, taking inc sts into patt.

Cont straight until sleeve meas 45 [45: 46: 46: 46] cm, ending with RS facing for next row.

Shape top

Keeping patt correct, cast off 7 [8: 8: 9: 9] sts at beg of next 2 rows. 80 [80: 82: 82: 84] sts.

Dec 1 st at each end of next 7 rows, then on foll 4 alt rows, then on every foll 4th row until 52 [52: 54: 54: 56] sts rem.

Work 1 row, ending with RS facing for next row.

Dec 1 st at each end of next and every foll alt row to 38 sts, then on foll 5 rows, ending with RS facing for next row.

Cast off rem 28 sts, dec 6 sts evenly.

MAKING UP

Press as described on the information page.

Join both shoulder seams using back stitch, or mattress stitch if preferred.

Left front band and collar

Using 3¼mm (US 3) needles cast on 4 sts.

Row 1 (RS): K4.

Row 2: sl 1, K3.

These 2 rows form patt.

Cont in patt until band, when slightly stretched, fits up left front opening edge to beg of front slope shaping, ending with RS facing for next row.

Shape for collar

Inc 1 st at beg of next and foll 24 alt rows, then on every foll 4th row until there are 51 sts.

Cont straight until collar, unstretched, fits up left front slope and across to centre back neck.

Cast off.

Slip stitch band in place.

Right front band and collar

Using 3¼mm (US 3) needles cast on 4 sts.

Row 1 (RS): sl 1, K3.

Row 2: K4.

These 2 rows form patt.

Complete to match left front band and collar, reversing shapings.

Slip stitch band in place, joining cast-off edges of collar sections at centre back neck.

Ties (make 2)
Using 3¼mm (US 3) needles cast on 8 sts.
Row 1 (RS): sl 1, K7.
Row 2: As row 1.
Rep these 2 rows until tie meas 102 cm.
Cast off.
See information page for finishing instructions, setting in sleeves using the set-in method and leaving a small opening in right side seam level with beg of front slope shaping. Attach ties to front opening edges level with beg of front slope shaping.

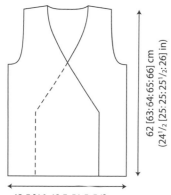

43.5 [46:48.5:51.5:54] cm
(17 [18:19:20¹/₂:21¹/₂] in)

62 [63:64:65:66] cm
(24¹/₂ [25:25:25¹/₂:26] in)

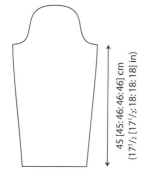

45 [45:46:46:46] cm
(17¹/₂ [17¹/₂:18:18:18] in)

YARN
RYC Luxury Cotton DK
A Crisp 253 2 x 50gm
B Tang 252 2 x 50gm

NEEDLES
1 pair 4mm (no 8) (US 6) needles

FINISHED SIZE
Completed scarf measures 8 cm (3 in) wide and 220 cm (86½in) long.

TENSION
22 sts and 30 rows to 10 cm measured over stocking stitch using 4mm (US 6) needles.

SCARF
Using 4mm (US 6) needles and yarn A cast on 22 sts.
Row 1 (WS): K2, P18, K2.
Row 2: Inc in first st, K18, K2tog, K1.
These 2 rows form patt.
Joining in colours as required, cont in patt in stripe sequence as folls:
Rows 3 to 12: Using yarn A.
Rows 13 to 24: Using yarn B.
These 24 rows form stripe sequence.
Rep last 24 rows 20 times more, then rows 1 to 12 again, ending after 12 rows using yarn A and with RS facing for next row.
Cast off.

MAKING UP
Press as described on the information page.

Georgina

YARN

	XS	S	M	L	XL
To fit bust	81	86	91	97	102 cm
	32	34	36	38	40 in

RYC Luxury Cotton DK

	9	10	10	11	12 x 50gm

(photographed in Marble 250)

NEEDLES

1 pair 3¼mm (no 10) (US 3) needles
1 pair 4mm (no 8) (US 6) needles
3¼mm (no 10) (US 3) circular needle
Cable needle

TENSION

28 sts and 30 rows to 10 cm measured over pattern using 4mm (US 6) needles.

SPECIAL ABBREVIATION

C4F = slip next 2 sts onto cable needle and leave at front of work, K2, then K2 from cable needle.

LEFT FRONT

Using 3¼mm (US 3) needles cast on 96 [100: 104: 108: 112] sts.
Row 1 (RS): P4 [4: 2: 2: 0], K0 [4: 0: 4: 0], *P2, K2tog, yfrn, P2, K4, rep from * to last 2 sts, P2.
Row 2: K2, P4, *K2, P2, K2, P4, rep from * to last 10 [4: 8: 2: 6] sts, (K2, P2) 1 [0: 1: 0: 1] times, K6 [4: 4: 2: 2].
Change to 4mm (US 6) needles.
Row 1 (RS): P4 [4: 2: 2: 0], (C4F) 0 [1: 0: 1: 0] times, *P2, yon, sl 1, K1, psso, P2, C4F, rep from * to last 2 sts, P2.
Row 2 and every foll alt row: K2, P4, *K2, P2, K2, P4, rep from * to last 10 [4: 8: 2: 6] sts, (K2, P2) 1 [0: 1: 0: 1] times, K6 [4: 4: 2: 2].
Row 3: P4 [4: 2: 2: 0], K0 [4: 0: 4: 0], *P2, K2tog, yfrn, P2, K4, rep from * to last 2 sts, P2.
Row 5: P4 [4: 2: 2: 0], K0 [4: 0: 4: 0], *P2, yon, sl 1, K1, psso, P2, K4, rep from * to last 2 sts, P2.
Row 7: As row 3.
Row 8: As row 2.
These 8 rows form patt.
Cont in patt for a further 10 rows, ending with RS facing for next row.
Shape front slope
Keeping patt correct, dec 1 st at end of next and

foll 40 [40: 39: 40: 38] alt rows, then on every foll 4th row until 54 [57: 61: 64: 69] sts rem.
Work 3 [3: 1: 1: 1] rows, ending with RS facing for next row. (Left front should meas 36 [37: 37: 38: 38] cm.)
Shape armhole
Keeping patt correct, cast off 7 [8: 9: 10: 11] sts at beg and dec 1 [1: 0: 0: 0] st at end of next row. 46 [48: 52: 54: 58] sts.
Work 1 row.
Dec 1 st at armhole edge of next 5 [7: 9: 11: 13] rows, then on foll 5 alt rows, then on 2 foll 4th rows **and at same time** dec 1 st at front slope edge on 3rd [3rd: next: next: next] and every foll 4th row. 28 [28: 29: 28: 30] sts.
Dec 1 st at front slope edge **only** on 4th [2nd: 2nd: 4th: 2nd] and every foll 4th row until 22 [22: 23: 23: 24] sts rem.
Cont straight until armhole meas 19 [19: 20: 20: 21] cm, ending with RS facing for next row.
Shape shoulder
Cast off 7 [7: 8: 8: 8] sts at beg of next and foll alt row.
Work 1 row.
Cast off rem 8 [8: 7: 7: 8] sts.

RIGHT FRONT

Using 3¼mm (US 3) needles cast on 96 [100: 104: 108: 112] sts.
Row 1 (RS): P2, K4, *P2, K2tog, yfrn, P2, K4, rep from * to last 10 [4: 8: 2: 6] sts, (P2, K2tog, yfrn) 1 [0: 1: 0: 1] times, P6 [4: 4: 2: 2].
Row 2: K4 [4: 2: 2: 0], P0 [4: 0: 4: 0], *K2, P2, K2, P4, rep from * to last 2 sts, K2.
Change to 4mm (US 6) needles.
Row 1 (RS): P2, C4F, *P2, yon, sl 1, K1, psso, P2, C4F, rep from * to last 10 [4: 8: 2: 6] sts, (P2, yon, sl 1, K1, psso) 1 [0: 1: 0: 1] times, P6 [4: 4: 2: 2].
Row 2 and every foll alt row: K4 [4: 2: 2: 0], P0 [4: 0: 4: 0], *K2, P2, K2, P4, rep from * to last 2 sts, K2.
Row 3: P2, K4, *P2, K2tog, yfrn, P2, K4, rep from * to last 10 [4: 8: 2: 6] sts, (P2, K2tog, yfrn) 1 [0: 1: 0: 1] times, P6 [4: 4: 2: 2].
Row 5: P2, K4, *P2, yon, sl 1, K1, psso, P2, K4, rep from * to last 10 [4: 8: 2: 6] sts, (P2, yon, sl 1, K1, psso) 1 [0: 1: 0: 1] times, P6 [4: 4: 2: 2].
Row 7: As row 3.

Row 8: As row 2.
These 8 rows form patt.
Cont in patt for a further 10 rows, ending with RS facing for next row.
Shape front slope
Keeping patt correct, dec 1 st at beg of next and foll 40 [40: 39: 40: 38] alt rows, then on every foll 4th row until 54 [57: 61: 64: 69] sts rem.
Complete to match left front, reversing shapings.

BACK

Using 3¼mm (US 3) needles cast on 124 [132: 140: 148: 156] sts.
Row 1 (RS): P4 [4: 2: 2: 0], K0 [4: 0: 4: 0], *P2, K2tog, yfrn, P2, K4, rep from * to last 10 [4: 2: 2: 6] sts, (P2, K2tog, yfrn) 1 [0: 1: 0: 1] times, P6 [4: 4: 2: 2].
Row 2: K4 [4: 2: 2: 0], P0 [4: 0: 4: 0], *K2, P2, K2, P4, rep from * to last 10 [4: 8: 2: 6] sts, (K2, P2) 1 [0: 1: 0: 1] times, K6 [4: 4: 2: 2].
Change to 4mm (US 6) needles.
Row 1 (RS): P4 [4: 2: 2: 0], (C4F) 0 [1: 0: 1: 0] times, *P2, yon, sl 1, K1, psso, P2, C4F, rep from * to last 10 [4: 8: 2: 6] sts, (P2, yon, sl 1, K1, psso) 1 [0: 1: 0: 1] times, P6 [4: 4: 2: 2].
Row 2 and every foll alt row: K4 [4: 2: 2: 0], P0 [4: 0: 4: 0], *K2, P2, K2, P4, rep from * to last 10 [4: 8: 2: 6] sts, (K2, P2) 1 [0: 1: 0: 1] times, K6 [4: 4: 2: 2].
Row 3: P4 [4: 2: 2: 0], K0 [4: 0: 4: 0], *P2, K2tog, yfrn, P2, K4, rep from * to last 10 [4: 8: 2: 6] sts, (P2, K2tog, yfrn) 1 [0: 1: 0: 1] times, P6 [4: 4: 2: 2].
Row 5: P4 [4: 2: 2: 0], K0 [4: 0: 4: 0], *P2, yon, sl 1, K1, psso, P2, K4, rep from * to last 10 [4: 8: 2: 6] sts, (P2, yon, sl 1, K1, psso) 1 [0: 1: 0: 1] times, P6 [4: 4: 2: 2].
Row 7: As row 3.
Row 8: As row 2.
These 8 rows form patt.
Cont in patt until back matches fronts to beg of armhole shaping, ending with RS facing for next row.
Shape armholes
Keeping patt correct, cast off 7 [8: 9: 10: 11] sts at beg of next 2 rows. 110 [116: 122: 128: 134] sts.
Dec 1 st at each end of next 5 [7: 9: 11: 13] rows, then on foll 5 alt rows, then on every foll 4th row until 86 [88: 90: 92: 94] sts rem.

Cont straight until back matches fronts to beg of shoulder shaping, ending with RS facing for next row.

Shape shoulders and back neck
Cast off 7 [7: 8: 8: 8] sts at beg of next 2 rows.
72 [74: 74: 76: 78] sts.
Next row (RS): Cast off 7 [7: 8: 8: 8] sts, patt until there are 12 [12: 11: 11: 12] sts on right needle and turn, leaving rem sts on a holder.
Work each side of neck separately.
Cast off 4 sts at beg of next row.
Cast off rem 8 [8: 7: 7: 8] sts.
With RS facing, rejoin yarn to rem sts, cast off centre 34 [36: 36: 38: 38] sts, patt to end.
Complete to match first side, reversing shapings.

MAKING UP
Press as described on the information page.
Join both shoulder seams using back stitch, or mattress stitch if preferred.
Front band
With RS facing and using 3¼mm (US 3) circular needle, beg and ending at cast-on edges, pick up and knit 15 sts up right front opening edge to beg of front slope shaping, 120 [122: 125: 127: 130] sts up right front slope to shoulder, 32 [34: 34: 36: 36] sts from back, 120 [122: 125: 127: 130] sts down left front slope to beg of front slope shaping, then 15 sts down left front opening edge. 302 [308: 314: 320: 326] sts.
Work in g st for 4 rows, ending with **WS** facing for next row.
Cast off knitwise (on **WS**).
Armhole borders (both alike)
With RS facing and using 3¼mm (US 3) needles, pick up and knit 94 [96: 102: 104: 110] sts evenly all round armhole edge.
Work in g st for 4 rows, ending with **WS** facing for next row.
Cast off knitwise (on **WS**).
Ties (make 2)
Using 3¼mm (US 3) needles cast on 4 sts.
Row 1 (RS): sl 1, K3.
Row 2: As row 1.
Rep these 2 rows until tie meas 102 cm.
Cast off.

See information page for finishing instructions, leaving small opening in left side seam level with beg of front slope shaping. Attach ties to front opening edges level with beg of front slope shaping. Make belt loop and attach to right side seam level with beg of front slope shaping.

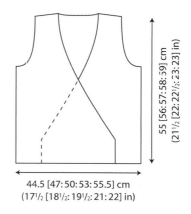

55 [56: 57: 58: 59] cm
(21½ [22: 22½: 23: 23] in)

44.5 [47: 50: 53: 55.5] cm
(17½ [18½: 19½: 21: 22] in)

Landscape

YARN

	XS	S	M	L	XL	
To fit bust	81	86	91	97	102	cm
	32	34	36	38	40	in

RYC Luxury Cotton DK

A Marble	250	3	3	3	4	4	x 50gm
B Damsel	251	2	2	2	3	3	x 50gm
C Crisp	253	1	1	2	2	2	x 50gm
D Broncho	256	2	2	2	2	2	x 50gm

NEEDLES

1 pair 3¼mm (no 10) (US 3) needles
1 pair 4mm (no 8) (US 6) needles

TENSION

22 sts and 30 rows to 10 cm measured over
stocking stitch using 4mm (US 6) needles.

STRIPE SEQUENCE

Beg with a K row, work in st st using colours as
folls:

Rows 1 to 4: Using yarn B.
Rows 5 to 8: Using yarn C.
Rows 9 to 12: Using yarn A.
Rows 13 to 16: Using yarn D.
Rows 17 to 22: Using yarn A.
Rows 23 to 26: Using yarn B.
Rows 27 to 32: Using yarn A.
Rows 33 and 34: Using yarn B.
Rows 35 and 36: Using yarn A.
Rows 37 to 52: As rows 33 to 36, 4 times.
Rows 53 to 56: Using yarn D.
Rows 57 to 60: Using yarn A.
Rows 61 to 64: Using yarn C.
Rows 65 to 68: Using yarn D.
Rows 69 to 72: Using yarn B.
Rows 73 and 74: Using yarn A.
Rows 75 to 78: Using yarn B.
Rows 79 to 82: Using yarn C.
Rows 83 to 86: Using yarn A.
Rows 87 to 90: Using yarn D.
Rows 91 to 94: Using yarn A.
Rows 95 to 98: Using yarn C.
Rows 99 to 102: Using yarn D.
Rows 103 to 106: Using yarn B.
Rows 107 onwards: Using yarn A.
These rows form stripe sequence.

BACK

Using 3¼mm (US 3) needles and yarn A cast on
82 [86: 94: 98: 106] sts.
Row 1 (RS): K2, *P2, K2, rep from * to end.
Row 2: P2, *K2, P2, rep from * to end.
These 2 rows form rib.
Work in rib for a further 2 rows, inc 0 [1: 0: 1: 0] st
at each end of last row and ending with RS facing
for next row. 82 [88: 94: 100: 106] sts.
Change to 4mm (US 6) needles.
Joining in and breaking off colours as required
and beg with a K row, cont in st st in stripe
sequence as folls:
Inc 1 st at each end of 13th and every foll 16th row
until there are 92 [98: 104: 110: 116] sts.
Cont straight until back meas 31 [32: 32: 33: 33] cm,
ending with RS facing for next row.
Shape armholes
Keeping stripes correct, cast off 5 [6: 6: 7: 7] sts
at beg of next 2 rows. 82 [86: 92: 96: 102] sts.
Dec 1 st at each end of next 5 [5: 7: 7: 9] rows,
then on foll 3 [4: 4: 5: 5] alt rows, then on foll
4th row. 64 [66: 68: 70: 72] sts.
Cont straight until armhole meas 19 [19: 20:
20: 21] cm, ending with RS facing for next row.
Shape shoulders and back neck
Cast off 3 sts at beg of next 2 rows.
58 [60: 62: 64: 66] sts.
Next row (RS): Cast off 3 sts, K until there are
6 [6: 7: 7: 8] sts on right needle and turn, leaving
rem sts on a holder.
Work each side of neck separately.
Cast off 4 sts at beg of next row.
Cast off rem 2 [2: 3: 3: 4] sts.
With RS facing, rejoin yarn to rem sts, cast off
centre 40 [42: 42: 44: 44] sts, K to end.
Complete to match first side, reversing shapings.

FRONT

Work as given for back until 12 [12: 12: 14: 14] rows
less have been worked than on back to beg of
shoulder shaping, ending with RS facing for next
row.
Shape neck
Next row (RS): K16 [16: 17: 18: 19] and turn,
leaving rem sts on a holder.
Work each side of neck separately.

Dec 1 st at neck edge of next 6 rows, then on foll
2 [2: 2: 3: 3] alt rows. 8 [8: 9: 9: 10] sts.
Work 1 row, ending with RS facing for next row.
Shape shoulder
Cast off 3 sts at beg of next and foll alt row.
Work 1 row.
Cast off rem 2 [2: 3: 3: 4] sts.
With RS facing, rejoin yarn to rem sts, cast off
centre 32 [34: 34: 34: 34] sts, K to end.
Complete to match first side, reversing shapings.

MAKING UP

Press as described on the information page.
Join right shoulder seam using back stitch, or
mattress stitch if preferred.
Neckband
With RS facing, using 3¼mm (US 3) needles and
yarn A, pick up and knit 14 [14: 14: 16: 16] sts
down left side of neck, 32 [34: 34: 34: 34] sts
from front, 14 [14: 14: 16: 16] sts up right side of
neck, then 48 [50: 50: 52: 52] sts from back.
108 [112: 112: 118: 118] sts.
Work in g st for 2 rows, ending with **WS** facing for
next row.
Cast off knitwise (on **WS**).
Join left shoulder and neckband seam.
Armhole borders (both alike)
With RS facing, using 3¼mm (US 3) needles and
yarn A, pick up and knit 96 [98: 102: 104: 108] sts
evenly all round armhole edge.
Work in g st for 2 rows, ending with **WS** facing for
next row.
Cast off knitwise (on **WS**).
See information page for finishing instructions.

50 [51: 52: 53: 54] cm
(19½ [20: 20½: 21: 21½] in)

42 [44.5: 47.5: 50: 52.5] cm
(16½ [17½: 18½: 19½: 20½] in)

Florence

YARN

	XS	S	M	L	XL	
To fit bust	81	86	91	97	102	cm
	32	34	36	38	40	in

RYC Luxury Cotton DK

| | 8 | 9 | 9 | 10 | 10 | x 50gm |

(photographed in Tang 252)

NEEDLES

1 pair 4mm (no 8) (US 6) needles
1 pair 4½mm (no 7) (US 7) needles

TENSION

30 sts and 30 rows to 10 cm measured over rib using 4mm (US 6) needles.

BODY (worked in one piece, beg at back hem edge)

Using 4mm (US 6) needles cast on 119 [127: 135: 143: 151] sts.
Row 1 (RS): P1, *K1, P1, rep from * to end.
Row 2: K1, *P1, K1, rep from * to end.
These 2 rows form rib.
Cont in rib until work meas 19 [20: 20: 21: 21] cm, ending with RS facing for next row.
Place markers at both ends of last row.
Cont in rib until work meas 36 [36: 38: 38: 40] cm from markers, ending with RS facing for next row.
Place second set of markers at both ends of last row.

Next row (RS): P1, inc once in each st to last st, P1.
236 [252: 268: 284: 300] sts.
Change to 4½mm (US 7) needles.
Next row: K1, *P2, K2, rep from * to last 3 sts, P2, K1.
Next row: P1, *K2, P2, rep from * to last 3 sts, K2, P1.
Rep last 2 rows until work meas 19 [20: 20: 21: 21] cm from second set of markers, ending with RS facing for next row.
Cast off loosely in patt.

SLEEVES (worked downwards)

With RS facing and using 4mm (US 6) needles, pick up and knit 75 [75: 79: 79: 83] sts evenly along one row-end edge of body between markers.
Beg with row 2, work in rib as given for body until sleeve meas 10 cm from pick-up row, ending with RS facing for next row.
Next row (RS): P1, inc once in each st to last st, P1.
148 [148: 156: 156: 164] sts.
Change to 4½mm (US 7) needles.
Next row: K1, *P2, K2, rep from * to last 3 sts, P2, K1.
Next row: P1, *K2, P2, rep from * to last 3 sts, K2, P1.
Rep last 2 rows until sleeve meas 15 cm from pick-up row, ending with RS facing for next row.
Cast off loosely in patt.

MAKING UP

Do NOT press.
Matching cast-on (back hem) and cast-off (front hem/neck) edges of body, join side and sleeve seams using back stitch, or mattress stitch if preferred.
See information page for finishing instructions.

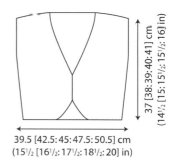

39.5 [42.5: 45: 47.5: 50.5] cm
(15½ [16½: 17½: 18½: 20] in)

37 [38: 39: 40: 41] cm
(14½ [15: 15½: 15½: 16] in)

15 cm
(6 in)

Vanessa

YARN

	XS	S	M	L	XL
To fit bust	81	86	91	97	102 cm
	32	34	36	38	40 in

RYC Luxury Cotton DK

	7	7	8	8	9 x 50gm

(photographed in Damsel 251)

NEEDLES

1 pair 3¼mm (no 10) (US 3) needles
1 pair 4mm (no 8) (US 6) needles
3¼mm (no 10) (US 3) circular needle

TENSION

22 sts and 30 rows to 10 cm measured over
stocking stitch using 4mm (US 6) needles.

BACK

Using 3¼mm (US 3) needles cast on 82 [86: 94:
98: 106] sts.
Row 1 (RS): K2, *P2, K2, rep from * to end.
Row 2: P2, *K2, P2, rep from * to end.
These 2 rows form rib.
Work in rib for 15 cm, inc 0 [1: 0: 1: 0] st at each end
of last row and ending with RS facing for next row.
82 [88: 94: 100: 106] sts.
Change to 4mm (US 6) needles.**
Beg with a K row, cont in st st, inc 1 st at each
end of 9th and every foll 8th row until there are
92 [98: 104: 110: 116] sts.
Work 7 [11: 11: 13: 13] rows, ending with RS facing
for next row. (Back should meas 31 [32: 32:
33: 33] cm.)
Shape armholes
Cast off 5 [6: 6: 7: 7] sts at beg of next 2 rows.
82 [86: 92: 96: 102] sts.
Dec 1 st at each end of next 3 [3: 5: 5: 7] rows, then
on foll 2 [3: 3: 4: 4] alt rows, then on foll 4th row.
70 [72: 74: 76: 78] sts.
Cont straight until armhole meas 20 [20: 21:
21: 22] cm, ending with RS facing for next row.
Shape shoulders and back neck
Cast off 6 [6: 7: 7: 7] sts at beg of next 2 rows.
58 [60: 60: 62: 64] sts.

Next row (RS): Cast off 6 [6: 7: 7: 7] sts, K until
there are 11 [11: 10: 10: 11] sts on right needle and
turn, leaving rem sts on a holder.
Work each side of neck separately.
Cast off 4 sts at beg of next row.
Cast off rem 7 [7: 6: 6: 7] sts.
With RS facing, rejoin yarn to rem sts, cast off
centre 24 [26: 26: 28: 28] sts, K to end.
Complete to match first side, reversing shapings.

FRONT

Work as given for back to **.
Divide for left front
Next row (RS): K22 [25: 28: 31: 34] and turn,
leaving rem sts on a holder.
Work each side separately.
Cast on and P 38 sts at beg of next row.
60 [63: 66: 69: 72] sts.
Shape front slope
Beg with a K row, cont in st st, dec 1 st at end of
next and foll 20 [20: 18: 19: 18] alt rows, then on
1 [2: 3: 3: 3] foll 4th rows **and at same time** inc
1 st at beg of 7th and 4 foll 8th rows.
43 [45: 49: 51: 55] sts.
Work 1 [1: 1: 1: 3] rows, ending with RS facing for
next row. (Left front should now match back to
beg of armhole shaping.)
Shape armhole
Cast off 5 [6: 6: 7: 7] sts at beg and dec 0 [0: 0:
0: 1] st at end of next row.
38 [39: 43: 44: 47] sts.
Work 1 row.
Dec 1 st at armhole edge of next 3 [3: 5: 5: 7] rows,
then on foll 2 [3: 3: 4: 4] alt rows, then on foll
4th row **and at same time** dec 1 st at front slope
edge on next [next: next: next: 3rd] and every foll
4th row.
29 [28: 30: 29: 30] sts.
Dec 1 st at front slope edge **only** on 2nd [4th: 2nd:
4th: 4th] and every foll 4th row until 19 [19: 20:
20: 21] sts rem.
Cont straight until left front matches back to beg
of shoulder shaping, ending with RS facing for
next row.

Shape shoulder

Cast off 6 [6: 7: 7: 7] sts at beg of next and foll alt
row.
Work 1 row.
Cast off rem 7 [7: 6: 6: 7] sts.
With RS facing, rejoin yarn to rem sts, K to end.
60 [63: 66: 69: 72] sts.
Next row (WS): Purl.
Shape front slope
Beg with a K row, cont in st st, dec 1 st at beg of
next and foll 20 [20: 18: 19: 18] alt rows, then on
1 [2: 3: 3: 3] foll 4th rows **and at same time** inc 1 st
at end of 7th and 4 foll 8th rows.
43 [45: 49: 51: 55] sts.
Complete to match left front, reversing shapings.

SLEEVES

Using 3¼mm (US 3) needles cast on 58 [58: 62:
62: 66] sts.
Work in rib as given for back for 10 rows, inc 0 [1:
0: 1: 0] st at each end of last row and ending with
RS facing for next row. 58 [60: 62: 64: 66] sts.
Change to 4mm (US 6) needles.
Beg with a K row, cont in st st, shaping sides by
inc 1 st at each end of 4th and every foll 3rd row
until there are 70 [72: 74: 76: 78] sts.
Work 3 rows, ending with RS facing for next row.
(Sleeve should meas 10 cm.)
Shape top
Cast off 5 [6: 6: 7: 7] sts at beg of next 2 rows.
60 [60: 62: 62: 64] sts.
Dec 1 st at each end of next 3 rows, then on foll
3 alt rows, then on every foll 4th row until 36 [36:
38: 38: 40] sts rem.
Work 1 row, ending with RS facing for next row.
Dec 1 st at each end of next and every foll alt row
to 28 sts, then on foll 3 rows, ending with RS
facing for next row.
Cast off rem 22 sts.

MAKING UP

Press as described on the information page.
Join both shoulder seams using back stitch, or
mattress stitch if preferred.

Front band

With RS facing and using 3¼mm (US 3) circular needle, beg at top of rib, pick up and knit 91 [94: 96: 99: 101] sts up right front slope to shoulder, 32 [34: 34: 36: 36] sts from back, then 91 [94: 96: 99: 101] sts down left front slope to cast-on edge. 214 [222: 226: 234: 238] sts.

Beg with row 2, work in rib as given for back for 4 rows, ending with WS facing for next row.

Cast off in rib (on **WS**).

Sew cast-on edge of left front and row-end edge of front band in place to top of rib behind right front. Sew other row-end edge of front band in place on RS. See information page for finishing instructions, setting in sleeves using the set-in method.

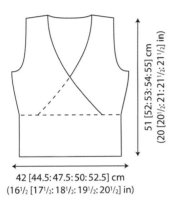

51 [52: 53: 54: 55] cm
(20 [20½: 21: 21½: 21½] in)

42 [44.5: 47.5: 50: 52.5] cm
(16½ [17½: 18½: 19½: 20½] in)

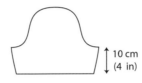

10 cm
(4 in)

Bohemian stripe

YARN

	XS	S	M	L	XL	
To fit bust	81	86	91	97	102	cm
	32	34	36	38	40	in

RYC Luxury Cotton DK

A Crisp	253	3	4	4	4	4	x 50gm
B Tang	252	3	3	3	4	4	x 50gm
C Broncho	256	3	3	3	4	4	x 50gm
D Marble	250	3	3	3	4	4	x 50gm

NEEDLES

1 pair 3¼mm (no 10) (US 3) needles
1 pair 4mm (no 8) (US 6) needles

TENSION

22 sts and 30 rows to 10 cm measured over
stocking stitch using 4mm (US 6) needles.

BACK

Using 3¼mm (US 3) needles and yarn A cast on
94 [102: 106: 114: 118] sts.
Row 1 (RS): K2, *P2, K2, rep from * to end.
Row 2: P2, *K2, P2, rep from * to end.
These 2 rows form rib.
Work in rib for a further 4 rows, dec 0 [1: 0: 1: 0] st
at each end of last row and ending with RS facing
for next row. 94 [100: 106: 112: 118] sts.
Change to 4mm (US 6) needles.
Joining in colours as required and beg with a K row,
cont in striped st st as folls:
Using yarn B, work 6 rows.
Using yarn C, work 6 rows.
Using yarn D, work 6 rows, dec 1 st at each end of
5th of these rows. 92 [98: 104: 110: 116] sts.
Using yarn A, work 6 rows.
These 24 rows form striped st st and beg side
seam shaping.
Cont in striped st st, shaping side seams by dec 1 st
at each end of next and foll 8th row, then on every
foll 6th row until 84 [90: 96: 102: 108] sts rem.
Work 9 rows, ending with RS facing for next row.

Inc 1 st at each end of next and every foll 8th row
until there are 94 [100: 106: 112: 118] sts.
Cont straight until back meas 35 [36: 36:
37: 37] cm, ending with RS facing for next row.
Shape armholes
Keeping stripes correct, cast off 5 [6: 6: 7: 7] sts
at beg of next 2 rows. 84 [88: 94: 98: 104] sts.
Dec 1 st at each end of next 5 [5: 7: 7: 9] rows, then
on foll 1 [2: 2: 3: 3] alt rows, then on foll 4th row.
70 [72: 74: 76: 78] sts.
Cont straight until armhole meas 20 [20: 21:
21: 22] cm, ending with RS facing for next row.
Shape shoulders and back neck
Cast off 6 [6: 7: 7: 7] sts at beg of next 2 rows.
58 [60: 60: 62: 64] sts.
Next row (RS): Cast off 6 [6: 7: 7: 7] sts, K until
there are 11 [11: 10: 10: 11] sts on right needle and
turn, leaving rem sts on a holder.
Work each side of neck separately.
Cast off 4 sts at beg of next row.
Cast off rem 7 [7: 6: 6: 7] sts.
With RS facing, rejoin appropriate yarn to rem sts,
cast off centre 24 [26: 26: 28: 28] sts, K to end.
Complete to match first side, reversing shapings.

FRONT

Work as given for back until 26 [26: 26: 28: 28]
rows less have been worked than on back to beg
of shoulder shaping, ending with RS facing for
next row.
Shape neck
Next row (RS): K28 [28: 29: 30: 31] and turn,
leaving rem sts on a holder.
Work each side of neck separately.
Dec 1 st at neck edge of next 4 rows, then on foll
4 [4: 4: 5: 5] alt rows, then on foll 4th row.
19 [19: 20: 20: 21] sts.
Work 9 rows, ending with RS facing for next row.
Shape shoulder
Cast off 6 [6: 7: 7: 7] sts at beg of next and foll alt
row.

Work 1 row.
Cast off rem 7 [7: 6: 6: 7] sts.
With RS facing, rejoin appropriate yarn to rem
sts, cast off centre 14 [16: 16: 16: 16] sts, K to end.
Complete to match first side, reversing shapings.

SLEEVES

Using 3¼mm (US 3) needles and yarn A cast on
50 [50: 50: 54: 54] sts.
Joining in colours as required, work in rib as
given for back in stripes as folls:
Using yarn A, work 2 rows.
Using yarn B, work 2 rows.
Using yarn C, work 2 rows.
Using yarn D, work 2 rows.
These 8 rows form stripe sequence.
Cont in rib in stripe sequence as set for a further
12 rows, inc 0 [0: 1: 0: 0] st at each end of last
row and ending with RS facing for next row.
50 [50: 52: 54: 54] sts.
Change to 4mm (US 6) needles.
Beg with a K row, cont in st st in stripe sequence
as set, shaping sides by inc 1 st at each end of
9th [7th: 7th: 7th: 7th] and every foll 10th [8th:
8th: 8th: 8th] row to 66 [56: 56: 58: 68] sts, then
on every foll 12th [10th: 10th: 10th: 10th] row until
there are 70 [72: 74: 76: 78] sts.
Cont straight until sleeve meas 46 [46: 47:
47: 47] cm, ending with RS facing for next row.
Shape top
Keeping stripes correct, cast off 5 [6: 6: 7: 7] sts
at beg of next 2 rows.
60 [60: 62: 62: 64] sts.
Dec 1 st at each end of next 3 rows, then on foll
4 alt rows, then on every foll 4th row until 34 [34:
36: 36: 38] sts rem.
Work 1 row, ending with RS facing for next row.
Dec 1 st at each end of next and every foll alt row
to 28 sts, then on foll 3 rows, ending with RS
facing for next row.
Cast off rem 22 sts.

MAKING UP

Press as described on the information page.
Join right shoulder seam using back stitch, or
mattress stitch if preferred.

Neckband

With RS facing, using 3¼mm (US 3) needles and
yarn D, pick up and knit 28 [28: 28: 31: 31] sts
down left side of neck, 14 [16: 16: 16: 16] sts from
front, 28 [28: 28: 31: 31] sts up right side of neck,
then 32 [34: 34: 36: 36] sts from back.
102 [106: 106: 114: 114] sts.
Joining in colours as required, work in rib as
given for back in stripes as folls:
Using yarn A, work 2 rows.
Using yarn C, work 2 rows.
Using yarn B, work 2 rows.

Using yarn A, work 2 rows.
Cast off in rib (on **WS**).

55 [56: 57: 58: 59] cm
(21½ [22: 22½: 23: 23] in)

42.5 [45.5: 48: 51: 53.5] cm
(16½ [18: 19: 20: 21] in)

See information page for finishing instructions,
setting in sleeves using the set-in method.

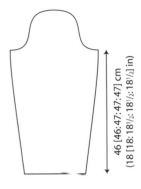

46 [46: 47: 47: 47] cm
(18 [18: 18½: 18½: 18½] in)

Artisan cuff

YARN
RYC Luxury Cotton DK
1 x 50gm
(photographed in Damsel 251)

NEEDLES
1 pair 3¾mm (no 9) (US 5) needles
Cable needle
2 double-pointed 3¾mm (no 9) (US 5) needles

EXTRAS
– 5 buttons. 5 round pearl beads
– ref P4 available from Creative Beadcraft Ltd.
15 cm of 4 cm wide petersham ribbon. Piece of
lining fabric 8 cm x 16 cm.

FINISHED SIZE
Completed cuff measures 4.5 cm (1¾ in) wide and
13.5 cm (5¼ in) long, excluding ties.

TENSION
22 sts and 30 rows to 10 cm measured over
stocking stitch using 4mm (US 6) needles.

SPECIAL ABBREVIATIONS
C4B = slip next 2 sts onto cable needle and leave
at back of work, K2, then K2 from cable needle;
C4F = slip next 2 sts onto cable needle and leave
at front of work, K2, then K2 from cable needle.

CUFF
Using 3¾mm (US 5) needles cast on 9 sts.
Rows 1 to 3: sl 1, K8.
Row 4 (WS): sl 1, K2, (M1, K1) 3 times, K3. 12 sts.

Row 5: sl 1, K11.
Row 6: sl 1, K1, P8, K2.
Row 7: sl 1, K1, C4B, C4F, K2.
Row 8: As row 6.
Rows 9 and 10: As rows 5 and 6.
Row 11: sl 1, K1, C4F, C4B, K2.
Row 12: As row 6.
Rows 13 to 44: As rows 5 to 12, 4 times.
Row 45: As row 5.
Row 46: sl 1, K2, (K2tog) 3 times, K3. 9 sts.
Row 47: sl 1, K8.
Cast off knitwise (on **WS**).

TIES (make 4)
Using double-pointed 3¾mm (US 5) needles cast
on 2 sts.
Row 1 (RS): K2, *without turning slip these 2 sts
to opposite end of needle and bring yarn to
opposite end of work pulling it quite tightly
across WS of work, K these 2 sts again, rep from
* until tie is 10 cm long, K2tog and fasten off.

MAKING UP
Press as described on the information page.
Attach ties to corners of cuff as in photograph.
Using photograph as a guide, attach buttons and
beads centrally on cables.
Trim petersham ribbon to same length as knitted
cuff section and sew in place to WS. Trim lining
fabric to same size as knitted cuff section, adding
seam allowance along all edges. Fold seam
allowance to WS, then slip stitch lining to WS of
cuff section.

Bloomsbury necklace and bracelet

YARN

RYC Luxury Cotton DK

A Slipper	254	1	x 50gm
B Damsel	251	1	x 50gm
C Broncho	256	1	x 50gm

NEEDLES

1 pair 4mm (no 8) (US 6) needles
2 double-pointed 4mm (no 8) (US 6) needles

DECORATION – 12 round pearl beads – ref P6 available from Creative Beadcraft Ltd.

FINISHED SIZE

Completed necklace is 64 cm (25 in) long, and bracelet is 40 cm (15½in) long.

TENSION

22 sts and 30 rows to 10 cm measured over stocking stitch using 4mm (US 6) needles.

FLOWERS

Using 4mm (US 6) needles and yarn A cast on 32 sts.
Row 1 (WS): K1, P30, K1.
Row 2: (K2tog) 16 times.
Row 3: (P2tog) 8 times.

Break yarn, leaving a fairly long end, and thread through rem 8 sts. Pull up tight and fasten off securely but do NOT cut yarn end yet.

Necklace only
Make a further 6 flowers in this way – 3 more using yarn A and 3 using yarn B.

Bracelet only
Make a further 4 flowers in this way – 2 more using yarn A and 2 using yarn B.

TIE

Using double-pointed 3¾mm (US 5) needles and yarn C cast on 2 sts.
Row 1 (RS): K2, *without turning slip these 2 sts to opposite end of needle and bring yarn to opposite end of work pulling it quite tightly across WS of work, K these 2 sts again, rep from * until tie is 64 cm long for necklace or 40 cm long for bracelet, K2tog and fasten off.

MAKING UP

Do NOT press.
Curl each flower round to form a double layer circle and secure in place. Using photograph as a guide and alternating colours, sew flowers centrally to tie, attaching a pearl bead at centre of each flower.

decorative yarn icon

Love pendant

YARN

RYC Luxury Cotton DK

1   x 50gm

(photographed in Marble 250)

NEEDLES

1 pair 3¾mm (no 9) (US 5) needles
2 double-pointed 3¾mm (no 9) (US 5) needles

EXTRAS – 24 round pearl beads – ref P6.
24 bugle beads – ref BB3 colour 1 Silver, all
beads available from Creative Beadcraft Ltd.
Piece of wadding 12 cm square.

FINISHED SIZE

Completed pendant is approx 9 cm (3½in) wide
and 9 cm (3½in) tall.

TENSION

22 sts and 30 rows to 10 cm measured over
stocking stitch using 4mm (US 6) needles.

PENDANT (make 2)

First section
Using 3¾mm (US 5) needles cast on 3 sts.
Row 1 (RS): (K1, M1) twice, K1. 5 sts.
Row 2 and every foll alt row: Purl.
Row 3: K1, M1, K3, M1, K1. 7 sts.
Row 5: K1, M1, K5, M1, K1. 9 sts.
Row 7: K1, M1, K7, M1, K1. 11 sts.
Row 8: Purl.**
Break yarn and leave sts on a holder.
Second section
Work as given for first section to **.

Join sections

Row 9 (RS): K1, M1, K next 9 sts of second section,
K tog last st of second section with first st of first
section, K next 9 sts of first section, M1, K1. 23 sts.
Row 11: Knit.
Row 13: K1, sl 1, K1, psso, K to last 3 sts, K2tog, K1.
Row 14: Purl.
Rep rows 13 and 14, 8 times more. 5 sts.
Row 31: K1, sl 1, K2tog, psso, K1. 3 sts.
Row 33: sl 1, K2tog, psso and fasten off.

TIE

Using double-pointed 3¾mm (US 5) needles cast
on 2 sts.
Row 1 (RS): K2, *without turning slip these 2 sts
to opposite end of needle and bring yarn to
opposite end of work pulling it quite tightly
across WS of work, K these 2 sts again, rep from
* until tie is 56 cm long and fasten off.

LOOP

Work as given for tie until strip is 3 cm long.

MAKING UP

Press as described on the information page.
Cut shape from wadding same size as knitted
heart shape. Sew heart shapes together around
entire outer edge, enclosing wadding between
layers. Using photograph as a guide, attach
3 pearl beads through all layers, and then
8 bugle beads around each pearl bead.
Sew rem pearl beads around outer edge.
Join ends of loop, then attach loop to back of
heart. Thread tie through loop.

Cherry bright brooch

YARN
RYC Luxury Cotton DK
          1   x 50gm
(photographed in Slipper 254)

NEEDLES
2.50mm (no 12) (US C2) crochet hook

EXTRAS – Brooch back.

FINISHED SIZE
Each cherry is approx 3.5 cm (1¼in) in diameter.

TENSION
First 3 rounds of first section measure 3.5 cm
(1¼in) in diameter on 2.50 mm crochet hook.

CROCHET ABBREVIATIONS
ch = chain; **ss** = slip stitch; **dc** = double crochet;
htr = half treble; **tr** = treble.

BROOCH
First section
Using 2.50mm (US C2) hook, make 4 ch and join
with a ss to form a ring.
Round 1 (RS): 1 ch (does NOT count as st),
8 dc into ring, ss to first dc. 8 sts.

Round 2: 1 ch (does NOT count as st), 2 dc into
each dc to end, ss to first dc.
16 sts.
Round 3: 1 ch (does NOT count as st), (1 dc into
next dc, 2 dc into next dc) 8 times, ss to first dc.
24 sts.
These 3 rounds complete first cherry.
Now work stalk and leaf as folls: 11 ch (to form
stalk), 8 ch (to form foundation ch of leaf), 1 dc
into 2nd ch from hook, 1 dc into each of next 5 ch,
3 dc into next ch, now working back along other
side of leaf foundation ch and keeping stalk at
WS of work, 1 dc into each of next 6 ch, 3 ch, 1 dc
into first dc, 1 htr into next dc, 1 tr into each of
next 3 dc, 1 htr into next dc, 1 dc into next dc, 1 ss
into next dc, 1 dc into next dc, 1 htr into next dc,
1 tr into each of next 3 dc, 1 htr into next dc, 1 dc
into next dc, ss to next dc.**
Fasten off.
Second section
Work as given for first section to **.
Work a ss into point of first section where leaf
meets stalk and fasten off.

MAKING UP
Do NOT press.
Attach brooch back to back of leaves.

 Gingerbread cottage bag

YARN

RYC Luxury Cotton DK

A Marble	250	3	x 50gm
B Slipper	254	1	x 50gm
C Crisp	253	1	x 50gm
D Broncho	256	1	x 50gm

Oddments of same yarn in 3 further colours
(E - Damsel 251, F – Char 257 and G – Tang 252)
for embroidery

NEEDLES

1 pair 4mm (no 8) (US 6) needles

EXTRAS – Piece of lining fabric 80 cm x 30 cm.
Same size piece of wadding. Sewing thread.
60 cm of 4 cm wide petersham ribbon.

TENSION

22 sts and 30 rows to 10 cm measured over
stocking stitch using 4mm (US 6) needles.

FINISHED SIZE

Completed bag measures 28 cm (11 in) wide and
23 cm (9 in) deep.

FRONT

Using 4mm (US 6) needles and yarn A cast on
61 sts.
Using the **intarsia** technique as described on the
information page, cont in patt from chart for
front, which is worked entirely in st st beg with
a K row, until all 56 rows of chart have been
completed, ending with RS facing for next row.
Break off contrasts and cont in st st using yarn D
only.
Shape for roof
Next row (RS): K2, K2tog, K to last 4 sts,
K2tog tbl, K2.
Next row: P2, P2tog tbl, P to last 4 sts, P2tog, K2.
Rep last 2 rows 6 times more, ending with RS
facing for next row.
Cast off rem 33 sts.

BACK

Using 4mm (US 6) needles and yarn A cast on
61 sts.
Using the **intarsia** technique as described on the
information page, cont in patt from chart for

back, which is worked entirely in st st beg with a
K row, until all 26 rows of chart have been
completed, ending with RS facing for next row.
Break off contrasts and cont in st st using yarn A
only.
Work 16 rows, ending with RS facing for next row.
Break off yarn A and join in yarn D.

Work 14 rows, ending with RS facing for next row.
Complete as given for front from beg of roof
shaping.

SIDE GUSSETS (make 2)

Using 4mm (US 6) needles and yarn A cast on
15 sts.

Front
Key   □ A   ■ B   ▨ C   ▨ D

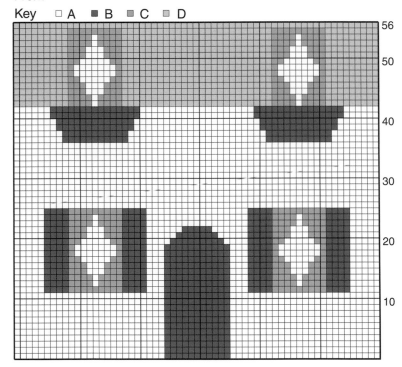

Back

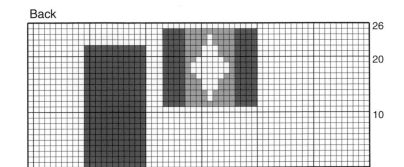

Beg with a K row, work in st st for 56 rows,
ending with RS facing for next row.
Cast off.

BASE

Using 4mm (US 6) needles and yarn A cast on
15 sts.
Beg with a K row, work in st st for 84 rows,
ending with RS facing for next row.
Cast off.

HANDLES (make 2)

Using 4mm (US 6) needles and yarn A cast on
21 sts.
Row 1 (RS): K5, sl 1 (for fold line), K9,
sl 1 (for fold line), K5.
Next row: Purl.
Rep these 2 rows until handle meas 30 cm,
ending with RS facing for next row.
Cast off.

MAKING UP

Press as described on the information page.
From lining fabric, cut out pieces same size as
front, back, side gussets and base, adding seam
allowance along all edges. From wadding, cut out
these pieces again, and then tack wadding to WS
of lining pieces.

Embroidery

Using photograph as a guide, embroider front
and back as folls: Using yarn F and back st,
outline doors, adding in lines to form "planks",
and then embroider french knot door knob. Using
yarn F and back st, outline windows, shutters and
window boxes, adding in lines to form "planks"
on shutters, and dividing each window into
4 window panes. Using yarn F, define edge of roof
by working a line of back st where section in yarn
D meets main section. Using yarn F and
photograph as a guide, embroider stem and
branches of creeper near front door. Using yarn G,
embroider single lazy daisy st leaves in window
boxes and over creeper. Using yarn E, embroider
french knot flowers on creeper and bullion knot
flowers in window boxes.
Join side gussets to front and back, matching
cast-on edges and cast-off edges of gussets to
beg of roof shaping. Sew base to cast-on edges
of front, back and side gussets. Join row-end edges
of handles. Cut petersham ribbon into 2 equal
lengths and thread through handles, securing it
at ends. Attach handles to inside of upper edge
of bag, positioning outer edges of handles level
with ends of cast-off rows of front and back.
Make up lining and wadding sections in same
way as knitted sections. Fold seam allowance to
WS around upper edge.
Slip lining inside bag and slip stitch in place
around upper opening edge.

Painter scarf

YARN
RYC Luxury Cotton DK

A Broncho	256	2	x 50gm
B Crisp	253	1	x 50gm
C Damsel	251	1	x 50gm
D Tang	252	1	x 50gm

NEEDLES
1 pair 4mm (no 8) (US 6) needles

FINISHED SIZE
Completed scarf measures 8 cm (3 in) wide and
228 cm (90 in) long.

TENSION
22 sts and 30 rows to 10 cm measured over
stocking stitch using 4mm (US 6) needles.

SCARF
Using 4mm (US 6) needles and yarn A cast on
27 sts.
Knit 1 row.
Join in yarn B and cont in patt as folls:
Row 1 (RS): Using yarn B, K1, sl 1, K1, psso, K9,
sl 2 as though to K2tog, K1, pass 2 slipped sts over,
K9, K2tog, K1. 23 sts.
Row 2: Using yarn B, K1, *P1, K4, (K1, yfwd, K1)
into next st, K4, rep from * once more, P1, K1.
27 sts.
These 2 rows form patt.
Joining in colours as required, cont in patt in
stripe sequence as folls:
Rows 3 and 4: Using yarn A.
Rows 5 and 6: Using yarn C.
Rows 7 and 8: Using yarn A.
Rows 9 and 10: Using yarn D.
Rows 11 and 12: Using yarn A.
These 12 rows form stripe sequence.
Cont in patt in stripe sequence as now set until
scarf meas approx 228 cm, ending after 2 rows
using yarn A and with RS facing for next row.
Cast off.

MAKING UP
Do NOT press.

Studio pendant

YARN
RYC Luxury Cotton DK

	1	x 50gm

(photographed in Crisp 253)

NEEDLES
2 double-pointed 3¾mm (no 9) (US 5) needles

EXTRAS
– 13 round pearl beads – ref P6. 1 large
clear round stone – ref PES2, and 8 petal shaped
coloured stones – ref PES8, selecting your own
colours from a wide colour range, all beads
available from Creative Beadcraft Ltd. 10 cm
circle of matching coloured felt. 80 cm of 12 mm
wide satin ribbon.

FINISHED SIZE
Completed pendant is approx 7 cm (2¾in) in
diameter.

TENSION
22 sts and 30 rows to 10 cm measured over
stocking stitch using 4mm (US 6) needles.

PENDANT
Using double-pointed 3¾mm (US 5) needles cast
on 2 sts.
Row 1 (RS): K2, *without turning slip these 2 sts
to opposite end of needle and bring yarn to
opposite end of work pulling it quite tightly
across WS of work, K these 2 sts again, rep from
* until strip is long enough, when coiled round,
to form a disk 7 cm in diameter, K2tog and
fasten off.

LOOP
Work as given for pendant until strip is 3 cm
long.

MAKING UP
Do NOT press.
Coil up pendant strip to form 7 cm diameter disk
and sew in place. Cut same size circle of felt and
sew to back of pendant. Using photograph as a
guide, attach stones to centre of coiled strip.
Sew pearl beads around outer edge.
Join ends of loop, then attach loop to back of
pendant. Thread ribbon through loop.

BELGIUM
Pavan, Meerlaanstraat 73,
B9860 Balegem (Oosterzele).
Tel: (32) 9 221 8594
Email: pavan@pandora.be

CANADA
Diamond Yarn,
9697 St Laurent,
Montreal,
Quebec, H3L 2N1.
Tel: (514) 388 6188

Diamond Yarn (Toronto),
155 Martin Ross, Unit 3, Toronto,
Ontario,M3J 2L9.
Tel: (416) 736 6111
Email: diamond@diamondyarn.com
Web: www.diamondyarns.com

FINLAND
Coats Opti Oy,
Ketjutie 3, 04220 Kerava
Tel: (358) 9 274 871
Fax: (358) 9 274 87330
Email: coatsopti.sales@coats.com

FRANCE
Elle Tricot : 8 Rue du Coq,
67000 Strasbourg.
Tel: (33) 3 88 23 03 13.
Email: elletricot@agat.net.
Web: www.elletricote.com

GERMANY
Wolle & Design,
Wolfshovener Strasse 76,
52428 Julich-Stetternich.
Tel: (49) 2461 54735.
Email: Info@wolleunddesign.de
Web: www.wolleunddesign.de

HOLLAND
de Afstap, Oude Leliestraat 12,
1015 AW Amsterdam.
Tel: (31) 20 6231445

HONG KONG
East Unity Co Ltd, Unit B2, 7/F Block B,
Kailey Industrial Centre,
12 Fung Yip Street, Chai Wan.
Tel: (852) 2869 7110
Fax: (852) 2537 6952
Email: eastuni@netvigator.com

ICELAND
Storkurinn, Laugavegi 59,
101 Reykjavik.
Tel: (354) 551 8258
Fax: (354) 562 8252
Email: malin@mmedia.is

ITALY
D.L. srl, Via Piave, 24 – 26,
20016 Pero, Milan.
Tel: (39) 02 339 10 180.

JAPAN
Puppy Co Ltd,
T151-0051,
3-16-5 Sendagaya,
Shibuyaku, Tokyo.
Tel: (81) 3 3490 2827
Email: info@rowan-jaeger.com

KOREA
Coats Korea Co Ltd,
5F Kuckdong B/D,
935-40 Bangbae-Dong,
Seocho-Gu, Seoul.
Tel: (82) 2 521 6262.
Fax: (82) 2 521 5181

NORWAY
Coats Knappehuset A/S,
Postboks 63,
2801 Gjovik.
Tel: (47) 61 18 34 00
Fax: (47) 61 18 34 20

SINGAPORE
Golden Dragon Store,
101 Upper Cross Street #02-51,
People's Park Centre.
Singapore 058357
Tel: (65) 65358454.
Email:gdscraft@hotmail.com

SOUTH AFRICA
Arthur Bales PTY,
PO Box 44644,
Linden 2104.
Tel: (27) 11 888 2401.

SPAIN
Oyambre, Pau Claris 145,
80009 Barcelona.
Tel: (34) 670 011957.
Email: comercial@oyambreonline.com

SWEDEN
Wincent, Norrtullsgatan 65,
113 45 Stockholm.
Tel: (46) 8 33 70 60
Fax: (46) 8 33 70 68
Email: wincent@chello.se
Web: www.wincentyarn.com

TAIWAN
Laiter Wool Knitting Co Ltd,
10-1 313 Lane, Sec 3,
Chung Ching North Road,
Taipei.
Tel: (886) 2 2596 0269.

U.S.A.
Westminster Fibers Inc,
4 Townsend West,
Suite 8, Nashua,
New Hampshire 03063.
Tel: (1 603) 886 5041 / 5043.
Email: rowan@westminsterfibers.com

U.K.
Rowan,
Green Lane Mill,
Holmfirth,
West Yorkshire,
HD9 2DX.
Tel: 01484 681881.
Email: mail@ryclassic.com
Web: www.ryclassic.com

For All Other Countries:
Please contact Rowan for stockists details.

BEAD STOCKISTS
Creative Beadcraft Ltd, Unit 2,
Asheridge Business Centre,
Asheridge Road, Chesham,
Buckinghamshire. HP5 2PT. England.
Telephone: + (44) 01494 778818
Email: bead@creativebeadcraft.co.uk
Website: www.creativebeadcraft.co.uk

Models – Rosie Williams and Alex Childs
Photography – Mark Scott
Styling – Tara Sloggett
Make up – Kj
Design layout – Nicky Downes

First published in Great Britain in 2006
by Rowan Yarns Ltd, Green Lane Mill,
Holmfirth, West Yorkshire, England, HD9 2DX

British Library Cataloguing in
Publication Data
Rowan Yarns
RYC Art
ISBN 1-904485-65-0